Queen Elizabeth II

The Life, Times, and Glorious 70 Year
Reign of England's Iconic Platinum
Monarch (1926-2022) - Her Fight for the
House of Windsor and Royal Palace
Papers Debacle

English Royal Press

Introduction

Do you want to know everything there is to know about Queen Elizabeth II?

Queen Elizabeth II died in 2022, at the age of ninety-six. She was the longest reigning British monarch in history and her death leaves a gaping hole in the British royal family. The queen's death sent the nation into mourning. The queen will be remembered for her long reign, her dedication to her country, and her love for her family.

This book tells the story of one of the most iconic and fascinating women in history. Elizabeth II has been a part of the British monarchy for over 70 years and her reign has seen some incredible changes. Read all about her life, times, and glorious reign in this comprehensive book.

In 1926, a young woman named Elizabeth Alexandra Mary was born to King George V and Queen Mary of England. She was the third child and second daughter of the royal couple, and she would go on to inherit the throne after her father's death in 1936. Elizabeth would reign as Queen of England for 70 years, becoming one of the longest-serving monarchs in English history.

She would also come to be one of the most beloved. Even early in her reign, Elizabeth proved herself to be a strong and capable leader, helping to guide the country through World War II. After the war ended, she set about rebuilding England's shattered economy and creating a new social welfare system. She also worked to strengthen the monarchy's ties to the people, visiting all corners of her country and earning the affectionate nickname "the People's Queen."

Throughout her long reign, Elizabeth has faced many challenges - including divorces, scandals, and even an attempted assassination. But she has always remained dignified and steadfast, earning the respect and admiration of her subjects. In 2002, Elizabeth became the longest-reigning British monarch in history, leaving a lasting legacy as one of England's most iconic monarchs.

Learn about all the Royal Palace Papers debacle that happened near the end of her reign. This was a huge controversy that made headlines around the world and revealed some interesting information about the queen and her family.

Table of Contents

Introduction 2

Table of Contents 5

Elizabeth II 7

First years 10

Legal heir to the Crown 12

World War II 14

Marriage 16

Reign 19

Continuing with the development of the Commonwealth of Nations 22

Silver Jubilee 26

1980s 29

1990s 32

Golden Jubilee 34

Diamond Jubilee and longevity 36

COVID-19 pandemic 40

Platinum Jubilee 43

Public perceptions and criticisms 44

Finance 46

Valuation and influence 47

In popular culture 49

Treatments, titles and weapons 50

Coat of arms and banners 51

Family.. 52

Elizabeth II

Elizabeth II of the United Kingdom (*Elizabeth Alexandra Mary*; London, April 21, 1926) is the current British monarch, as well as sovereign of fourteen other independent states constituted as a kingdom and forming part of the Commonwealth of Nations: United Kingdom, Canada, Australia, New Zealand, Jamaica, Jamaica, Bahamas, Grenada, Papua New Guinea, Solomon Islands, Tuvalu, Saint Lucia, Saint Vincent and the Grenadines, Belize, Antigua and Barbuda, and Saint Kitts and Nevis.

She is the leading political figure in the fifty-four member countries of the Commonwealth of Nations. In her specific role as monarch of the United Kingdom, she is also the supreme ruler of the Church of England. Her political role covers large areas, she has significant constitutional functions and acts as the focus of the national unity of the British people and as a representative of her nation to the world. [1]

She was born in London, being the eldest daughter of the Duke and Duchess of York (later King George VI and Queen Elizabeth) and was educated at home by private tutors. [2]Her father ascended the throne in 1936 after the abdication of his brother Edward VIII. [3]She began to carry out public functions during the Second World War,[4] serving in the Auxiliary Territorial Service, the female branch of the British Army at the time. When her father died in 1952, she became head of the Commonwealth of Nations and queen of the seven independent countries belonging to it: United Kingdom, Canada, Australia, New Zealand, South Africa, Pakistan and Ceylon. Her coronation celebration in 1953 was the first to be televised. [5]Between 1956 and 2021, half of her kingdoms, including South Africa, Pakistan, Ceylon (later renamed Sri Lanka) and Barbados, gained their independence and became republics.

In 1947 she married Prince Philip of Greece and Denmark, with whom she had four children: Charles, Anne, Andrew and Edward. In 1992, a year that Elizabeth called *annus horribilis* ('horrible year'),[6] Charles and Andrew separated from their wives, Anne divorced and a serious fire destroyed part of Windsor Castle. Rumors about the marital situation of Charles and Diana, Princess of Wales continued and the two divorced in 1996. The following year, Diana died in a car accident in Paris and the media criticized the royal family for remaining in seclusion in the days leading up to her funeral. [7]Since 2007, she has been the longest-reigning monarch in British history, surpassing her great-great-grandmother, Queen Victoria. [8]She is one of the longest reigning monarchs in history and, since September 2015, the longest reigning British monarch after surpassing Queen Victoria once again. [9]

His silver, gold, diamond, sapphire and platinum jubilees were celebrated in 1977, 2002, 2012, 2017 and 2022 respectively. [10]

On April 9, 2021, her husband, Prince Philip, Duke of Edinburgh, died two months before his 100th birthday, and 12 days before her 95th birthday. Elizabeth II's marriage is the longest-lasting in the history of the royal family, the couple was together for more than 74 years.

The Commonwealth Realms celebrated, between June 2 and 6, 2022, in the so-called *Jubilee Days*, the platinum jubilee, an event that commemorated the 70th anniversary of the reign of Elizabeth II, on February 6, 2022.

First years

Elizabeth was the first daughter of Prince Albert, Duke of York (later King George VI) and his wife Elizabeth, Duchess of York (later Queen Elizabeth). Her father was the second son of King George V and Queen Mary, and her mother was the youngest daughter of Scottish aristocrat Claude Bowes-Lyon, 14th Earl of Strathmore and Kinghorne. Elizabeth was born by caesarean section at 2:40 GMT on April 21, 1926 at her maternal grandfather's London home at 17 Bruton Street, Mayfair. [11][12] He then resided briefly in a home acquired by his parents shortly after his birth at 145 Piccadilly in London and at the White Lodge residence in Richmond Park. [13]On May 29, 1926, the Archbishop of York, Cosmo Lang, baptized her under the Anglican religion in the private chapel at Buckingham Palace (destroyed during the bombing of London in World War II). [14][note 1] She was named "Elizabeth" after her mother, "Alexandra" after George V's mother (her paternal great-grandmother), who had died six months earlier, and "Mary" after her paternal grandmother. [15]In private, she was called "Lilibet". [16]George V was very fond of his granddaughter and during her serious illness in 1929, her regular visits lifted his spirits and aided his recovery, as credited by the public press and his later biographers. [17]

Her only sister was Princess Margaret, born in 1930. Both were educated at home under the supervision of their mother and Marion Crawford, their governess, informally called "Crawfie". [2]Lessons concentrated mainly on history, language, literature and music. [18]To the dismay of the royal family,[19] Crawford later published a biographical book about Elizabeth and Margaret's early years entitled *The*

Little Princesses. The book describes Elizabeth's love of horses and dogs, her discipline and her attitude of responsibility. [20]Others echoed such observations: Winston Churchill described Elizabeth when she was two years old as "a character. She has an air of authority and thoughtfulness surprising for a child." [21]Her cousin Margaret Rhodes described her as "a cheerful child, but, fundamentally, sensitive and well-behaved." [22]

Legal heir to the Crown

As a granddaughter of the monarch, Elizabeth's full title at
birth was *Her Royal Highness* Princess Elizabeth of York.
She was third in line to the throne behind her uncle,
Edward, Prince of Wales, and her father. Although her birth
produced public interest, it was not expected that she
would be queen considering that the Prince of Wales was
young and therefore, many believed that she would marry
and have children. [23]In 1936, when her grandfather died
and Edward succeeded him as king, Elizabeth became
second in line to the throne after her father. That same
year, Edward abdicated after the constitutional crisis
caused by his proposal of marriage to Wallis Simpson, an
American divorcee. [3]Although he could legally marry,
ministers advised against it, as the people would never
accept her as queen; as a constitutional monarch Edward
was obliged to accept the ministers' advice. George V had
expressed his views about his eldest son: "I pray to God
that my eldest son may never marry or have children, so
that nothing may come between Bertie and Lilibet and the
throne". [24]With the abdication of Edward VIII, Elizabeth's
father became king and she became the legal heir with the
title of *Her Royal Highness* Princess Elizabeth. [25]

Elizabeth was tutored in constitutional history by Henry
Marten, the rector of Eton College,[26] and learned French
with the help of several governesses. [27]The Girl Guides
scouting movement, Buckingham Palace's first troupe, was
formed specifically so that Elizabeth could socialize with
girls her own age. [28]Later, she joined the Sea Ranger
youth organization. [27]

In 1939, Elizabeth's parents toured Canada and the United States. As in 1927, when they toured Australia and New Zealand, Elizabeth remained in Britain, as the king thought she was too young for public visits. [29]Elizabeth "looked tearful" when her parents left. [30]They communicated by letters regularly, and on May 18, Elizabeth and her parents made the first real transatlantic telephone call.

World War II

From September 1939, with the outbreak of World War II, Elizabeth and her younger sister, Margaret, remained at Balmoral Castle, Scotland, until Christmas 1939, when they moved to Sandringham House (in Norfolk). [31]From February to May 1940, they resided at Royal Lodge, until they were moved to Windsor Castle, where they remained for most of the next five years. [32]The suggestion by the prominent politician Lord Hailsham[33] that the princesses be taken to Canada was rejected by Elizabeth's mother, who declared, "The girls will not go without me. I will not leave the king. And the king will never leave." [34]At Windsor, the princesses performed pantomimes at Christmas in aid of the Queen's Wool Fund, which purchased the yarn needed to make military garments. [35]In 1940, 14-year-old Elizabeth made her first radio broadcast for the BBC *Children's Hour* program, where she stated: [36]

In 1943, at the age of 16, Elizabeth made her first solo public appearance on a visit to the Grenadier Guards, of which she had been appointed colonel-in-chief the previous year. [37]As her 18th birthday approached, the laws were changed so that she could act as one of five state councilors in the event of her father's incapacity or absence abroad, as happened when she visited Italy in July 1944.[4]In February 1945, she joined the Women's Auxiliary Territorial Service as an honorary *Second Subaltern* with service number 230873.[38] She trained as a driver and mechanic,[39] and was promoted to honorary *Junior Commander* five months later. [40]

During the war, plans were developed to stifle Welsh nationalism by affiliating Elizabeth more closely with Wales. [41]Welsh politicians promoted the proposal that she become Princess of Wales on her 18th birthday. The idea was supported by the Home Secretary, Herbert Morrison, but was rejected by the king because he considered it a title that belonged solely to the wife of the Prince of Wales. Moreover, the latter had always been the heir (usually the sovereign's eldest son) and Elizabeth was only the legal heir and could be replaced in the line of succession if the king had a son. [42]In 1946, she was included in the Welsh Gorsedd community of Bards in the National Eisteddfod of Wales. [43]

At the end of the war, on Victory in Europe Day, Elizabeth and her sister dispersed into the crowds anonymously to celebrate in the streets of London. Later, she said in an interview; "We asked our parents if we could go out and watch the celebration on our own. I remember we were terrified that we would be recognized...I remember the lines of strangers linking arms and walking down Whitehall, we were all just overcome by a tide of happiness and relief." [44]Two years later, the princess made her first overseas tour when she accompanied her parents to southern Africa. During the tour, in a special broadcast to the Commonwealth on her twenty-first birthday, she promised, "I declare before you that my whole life, whether long or short, will be devoted to our service and to the service of our great imperial family to which we all belong." [45]

Marriage

Elizabeth met her future husband, Prince Philip of Greece and Denmark, in 1934 and saw him again in 1937.[46] After another meeting at Britannia Royal Naval College in July 1939, Elizabeth - just 13 years old - fell in love with Philip, son of Prince Andrew of Greece and Alice of Battenberg, and they began communicating by letters. [47]They were married on November 20, 1947 at Westminster Abbey. They are niece and uncle in the third degree on the side of King Christian IX of Denmark and third cousins on the side of Queen Victoria. Before the marriage, Philip renounced his Greek and Danish titles, converted from Greek Orthodoxy to Anglicanism and adopted the designation Lieutenant Philip Mountbatten, taking the surname of his mother's British family. [48]Just before the wedding, he was appointed Duke of Edinburgh and received the treatment of *His Royal Highness*. [49]

The marriage was not without controversy: Philip lacked financial ability, came from abroad (through a British subject), and had sisters who had married Nazi-related German nobles. [50]Marion Crawford wrote: "Some of the king's advisers did not think him good enough for her. He was a prince without a home or kingdom....". [51]While Elizabeth's mother initially opposed the relationship,[52] later told biographer Tim Heald that Philip was an "English gentleman." [53]

Elizabeth and Philip received 2500 wedding gifts from all over the world,[54] even though Britain had not yet recovered from the devastation of the war. Elizabeth even needed ration coupons to purchase the materials for her wedding dress, designed by the couturier Norman Hartnell[55] in ivory satin and decorated with silver thread, tulle embroidery and 10,000 white pearls imported directly from America. [56]Her bouquet of white orchids and myrtle, taken from the bush that Queen Victoria had planted after her wedding, was placed on the tomb of the unknown soldier, an act that her mother had also performed in 1923.[57] After the religious ceremony, a meal was offered to the guests at Buckingham Palace. [56]

In post-war Britain, it was not acceptable for German relations of the Duke of Edinburgh's family to be invited to the wedding, including his three sisters. [58]One notable absentee was Edward, the former king, who was not invited, while his sister, Princess Mary, was absent due to health problems. Ronald Storrs claimed he did not attend in protest at his brother's exclusion. [59]

The ceremony was officiated by the Archbishop of Canterbury and the Archbishop of York. [60]Eight bridesmaids were present, including Elizabeth's cousin Margaret Rhodes. The wedding was attended by more than 2,000 guests and BBC radio broadcast the celebration live. Prime Minister Winston Churchill called the celebration "a splash of color on the hard road ahead. Michael Parker, Philip's friend and private secretary, declared that "Philip was terribly bored with all the obligations of royalty, all those formal engagements and handshakes.... It wasn't his thing." [61]

Elizabeth gave birth to their first son, Prince Charles, on November 14, 1948, less than a month after George VI issued a royal patent, which allowed his children to use the treatment and title of prince or princess. [62]The couple had a daughter in 1950, Princess Anne. [63]

After the wedding, the royal couple resided at Windlesham Moor near Windsor Castle until July 4, 1949,[54] when they settled at Clarence House in London. On repeated occasions between 1949 and 1951, the Duke of Edinburgh was posted to the British protectorate of Malta as an officer in the Royal Navy. He and his wife lived intermittently for several months in the Maltese village of Gwardamangia, in Villa Gwardamangia and in the rented house of Philip's uncle, Lord Mountbatten. However, their children remained in the United Kingdom.

Reign

Succession and coronation

In December 1936, King Edward VIII of the United Kingdom abdicated in order to marry the divorced commoner Wallis Simpson of the United States, making his younger brother Albert the new monarch with the name of George VI of the United Kingdom and his niece Elizabeth the crown princess. From then on, young but determined, she began to shape her image as a future queen. George VI's health worsened considerably during 1951 (he was diagnosed with lung cancer in September,[65] suffered an arterial obstruction and underwent a lung resection)[66] and Elizabeth soon replaced him in virtually all public events. In October of that year, he toured Canada and visited U.S. President Harry S. Truman in Washington; on the trip, his private secretary, Martin Charteris, carried with him the declaration of accession, in case the king died during the tour. [67]In early 1952, Elizabeth and Philip departed for a tour of Australia, New Zealand, and Kenya. On February 6, 1952, when they had barely arrived at Sagana Lodge - their residence in the latter country - and after spending a night at the Treetops Hotel, they received the news of the death of Elizabeth's father. [68]Philip was charged with conveying the fact to the new queen. Charteris asked her to choose a name for the position; she chose Elizabeth, "of course," as she declared. [69]She was proclaimed queen and the royal retinue hurried back to the United Kingdom,[70] where the marriage was transferred to Buckingham Palace. [71]

With Elizabeth's accession, it seemed likely that the royal household would bear her husband's name. Lord Mountbatten thought it would thereafter become Mountbatten House, as Elizabeth would have taken Philip's surname after the marriage. However, Queen Mary and British Prime Minister Winston Churchill were in favor of keeping the name of the House of Windsor. The Duke, for his part, complained: "I am the only man in the country who is not allowed to give his surname to his own children". [72]In 1953, after the death of Queen Mary on March 24, 1953 and the resignation of Churchill in 1955, the surname *Mountbatten-Windsor* was adopted for Philip and Elizabeth's male descendants who did not hold royal titles. [73]

In the midst of preparations for the coronation, Princess Margaret informed her sister that she wanted to marry Peter Townsend, a divorced commoner 16 years her senior with two children from his previous marriage. The queen asked them to wait a year; in the words of Martin Charteris, "the queen was naturally sympathetic to the princess, but I think she thought - rather, she hoped - that at some point, the courtship would end." [74]High-ranking politicians were against the union, and the Church of England did not allow marriage after divorce. If Margaret entered into a civil marriage, she would have to give up her right of succession. [75]Finally, she decided to abandon her plans with Townsend. [76]In 1960, she married Antony Armstrong-Jones, 1st Earl of Snowdon. The couple divorced in 1978 and Margaret never remarried. [77]

Despite the death of Queen Mary, ten weeks before the coronation, the coronation was held at Westminster Abbey on June 2, 1953. Before her death, Queen Mary had made it clear that in the event of her death the coronation was not to be postponed. The entire ceremony, with the exception of the anointing and communion, was televised for the first time in British history and the coverage was instrumental in boosting the medium's popularity; the number of television licenses in the UK doubled to 3 million,[78] and more than 20 million viewers watched the event at their friends' or neighbors' homes. [79]In North America, just under 100 million viewers watched the broadcasts. [80]Elizabeth wore a dress commissioned from Norman Hartnell embroidered, according to his instructions, with the floral emblems of the Commonwealth countries:[81] English Tudor rose, Scottish thistle, Welsh leek, Irish shamrock, Australian golden wattle, Canadian maple leaf, New Zealand silver fern, South African protea, sacred lotus for India and Ceylon, and wheat, cotton and jute for Pakistan. [82]Elizabeth II is the longest reigning monarch in British history. Only five other kings and queens have reigned the United Kingdom for more than 50 years: Victoria (63 years), George III (59 years), Henry III (56 years), Edward III (50 years) and James VI of Scotland (James I of England) (58 years).

Continuing with the development of the Commonwealth of Nations

Throughout her life, Elizabeth witnessed the progressive transformation of the British Empire into the Commonwealth of Nations. By the time of her ascension to the throne in 1952, her role as nominal head of several independent states was already established. [83]Between 1953 and 1954, the Queen and her husband embarked on a six-month tour around the world, becoming the first Queen of Australia and New Zealand to visit these countries. [84][85] During the tour, the approaching crowds were immense; it was estimated that three-quarters of the Australian population watched Elizabeth pass by. [86]Throughout her reign, she has made numerous state visits to other countries, especially those belonging to the Commonwealth of Nations, making her the most traveled monarch in the history of the United Kingdom. [87]

In 1956, French Prime Minister Guy Mollet and British Prime Minister *Sir* Anthony Eden discussed the possibility of including France in the Commonwealth of Nations. The proposal was never accepted, and the following year France signed the Treaties of Rome, which provided for the creation of the European Economic Community, the forerunner of the European Union. [88]In November 1956, the United Kingdom and France invaded Egypt in an unsuccessful attempt to recover the Suez Canal. Controversy erupted when Lord Mountbatten claimed that the Queen opposed the invasion, while Eden denied the claim and eventually resigned two months later. [89]

The absence of a formal mechanism in the Conservative Party for the election of a leader meant that, following Eden's resignation, it was up to the queen to decide who would sit on the committee to form the new government. Eden recommended that Elizabeth consult with Lord Salisbury (the Lord President of the Council). Lord Salisbury and Lord Kilmuir (the Lord Chancellor) consulted the Cabinet, Winston Churchill and the legislators of the 1922 Committee's Governing Council; as a result, Elizabeth appointed her recommended candidate: Harold Macmillan. [90]

In 1957, the Suez crisis and the election of Eden's successor led to the first major criticism of the queen. In a publication edited and produced by Lord Altrincham,[91] he accused her of "having lost touch". [92]Altrincham was denounced by several public figures and physically assaulted by a member of the public angered by his comments. [93]Six years later in 1963, Macmillan resigned and recommended to the queen that she appoint Earl Home as prime minister, advice she followed. [94]He would also again be the target of criticism for appointing the prime minister on the advice of a small group of ministers, or just one of them. [94]In 1965, the Conservatives opted for a formal mechanism for choosing a leader, which exempted her from participating. [95]

In 1957, Elizabeth made a state visit on behalf of the Commonwealth of Nations to the United States, where she addressed the United Nations General Assembly. On the same tour, she opened the twenty-third parliamentary session of Canada, becoming the first Canadian monarch to do so. [96]Two years later, he visited the United States again as Canada's representative. [96][97] In 1961, he toured

23

Cyprus, India, Pakistan, Nepal and Iran. [98]During a visit to Ghana the same year, she dismissed fears about her safety, even though President Kwame Nkrumah, who had replaced her as head of state, was a target for assassins. [99]Harold Macmillan wrote: "The queen has always been absolutely resolute.... She is impatient with the attitude they take toward her as if she were...a movie star...she really has 'the heart and stomach of a man'...she loves duty and what it means to be a queen." [99]In 1959, along with President Dwight D. Eisenhower, she officially opened the St. Lawrence Seaway, a system of locks, conduits and canals that allows ocean-going vessels to travel from the Atlantic Ocean to Lake Superior. [100]

Her pregnancies of Princes Andrew and Edward in 1959 and 1963, respectively, were the only two occasions on which the Queen was absent from the opening ceremonies of the United Kingdom's parliamentary sessions. [101]In addition to performing her traditional acts, she also instituted new habits. Her first royal walk, surrounded by members of the general public, took place during a tour of Australia and New Zealand in 1970. [102]

The 1960s and 1970s were marked by an acceleration of decolonization in Africa and the Caribbean. More than 20 countries gained independence from the United Kingdom as part of a planned transition to self-government. In 1965, however, Rhodesia's prime minister, Ian Smith, self-proclaimed independence despite opposition from black movements, withdrawing it from the Commonwealth of Nations. Although the Queen dismissed Smith in a formal declaration and the international community applied sanctions against Rhodesia, Smith's regime endured for more than a decade. [103]

In February 1974, British Prime Minister Edward Heath called a general election in the middle of the Queen's tour of the Pacific Rim and had to interrupt his visit to fly back to Britain. [104]The inconclusive result of the election meant that Heath, whose Conservative Party had the most votes but not an absolute majority, could remain in office if a coalition was formed with the Liberals. Heath resigned when discussions on forming a cooperative government failed, after the queen talked with the opposition leader, Labour's Harold Wilson, to form a government. [105]

A year later, with the Australian constitutional crisis of 1975, Australian Prime Minister Gough Whitlam was removed from office by Governor-General *Sir* John Kerr after the Senate rejected Whitlam's budget proposals. [106]As Whitlam had the majority of votes in the House of Representatives, President Gordon Scholes contacted Elizabeth to reverse Kerr's decision. The queen refused, stating that she would not intervene in decisions reserved for the governor general as set out in the Australian Constitution. [107]This crisis fueled Australian republicanism. [106]

Silver Jubilee

In 1977, Elizabeth celebrated her silver jubilee as queen, for which parties and events were held throughout the United Kingdom, many of which coincided with national tours and trips to Commonwealth countries. The celebrations reaffirmed the Queen's popularity, despite negative press reports that were more focused on Princess Margaret's separation from her husband. [108]In February 1977, a number of religious ceremonies were held throughout the month. On May 17, she made a tour through Glasgow and in turn, made other state trips to Western Samoa, Australia, New Zealand, Tonga, Fiji, Tasmania, Papua New Guinea, Canada and India. In the end, it was estimated that the Queen and her husband had traveled more than 56,000 miles. [109]On June 6, 1977, the celebrations for her silver jubilee as Queen began and a day later, she rode in the Gold State Coach to St. Paul's Cathedral in London for a thanksgiving service attended by heads of state from around the world and retired British prime ministers. [109]He then attended a luncheon at Guildhall with his family, where he delivered a speech, and on his return to Buckingham Palace he waved from the balcony to the crowds present. An estimated 500 million people watched the procession on television. [109]

In 1978, Elizabeth received the communist dictator of Romania, Nicolae Ceaușescu, on a state visit. [110]By the following year, Elizabeth's life was marked by two events: the unmasking of Anthony Blunt - the curator of the queen's pictorial works - as a communist spy, and the assassination of her uncle-in-law Lord Mountbatten by the Provisional Irish Republican Army. [111]

According to Paul Martin, in the late 1970s Elizabeth was concerned that "the Crown had little meaning" for Canadian Prime Minister Pierre Trudeau. [112]Tony Benn said that the Queen was "disappointed" with Trudeau;[112] on the other hand, these statements seemed to be confirmed by his attitude towards the Queen, for example, when he slid down the railings of Buckingham Palace and performed some pirouettes behind Elizabeth in 1977, or when he removed some royal symbols of Canada during his term of office. [112]In 1980, some Canadian politicians arrived in London to discuss the repatriation of the Canadian constitution and found Elizabeth "better informed about Canada's constitutional case than any of the British politicians or bureaucrats." [112]She was interested in the constitutional debate after the failure of Bill C-60, which had affected her role as head of state. [112]Repatriation had stifled the role of the British Parliament in the Canadian constitution, but the monarchy was retained. Trudeau said in his memoirs, "The queen favored my attempt to reform the constitution. She always impressed me not only by the grace she emitted in public at all times, but also by the wisdom she displayed during private conversation."

1980s

During the 1981 *Trooping the Colour* ceremony and just six weeks before the wedding of Prince Charles and Diana Spencer, six shots were fired at the Queen from a short distance as she rode to The Mall on her horse "Burmese". Police later discovered that the bullets fired were rubber bullets. The 17-year-old assailant, Marcus Sargeant, was sentenced to five years in prison and released after three. [114]The queen's calmness and riding skills were widely praised. [115]From April to September of that year, the queen was especially proud[116] and somewhat anxious[117] of her son Andrew, as he served in the British Armed Forces during the Falklands War. On July 9 the following year, when Elizabeth awoke in her room at Buckingham Palace, she found an intruder, Michael Fagan, standing at the foot of the bed. She remained calm as she contacted the central police department, and talked with Fagan until the authorities arrived seven minutes later. [118]Although he hosted President Ronald Reagan at Windsor Castle in 1982 and visited his California ranch in 1983, he was upset when the U.S. government ordered the invasion of Grenada, one of his Caribbean kingdoms, without his prior consent. [119]Pope John Paul II's 1982 visit was the first visit by a Catholic pope to the United Kingdom in 450 years.

During the 1980s, the great media interest in the views and private lives of the British royal family led to a series of sensationalist stories within the press, although not all of them were true. [120]Newspaper editor Donald Trelford wrote in *The Observer* on September 21, 1986: "The royal television serial has reached such a degree of public interest that the boundary between fact and fiction has been lost sight of. It is not fair that some papers do not corroborate claims or accept denials: they do not care whether the stories are true or not." *citation needed* It was reported, including in the July 20, 1986 edition of *The Sunday Times*, that Elizabeth was concerned that British Prime Minister Margaret Thatcher's economic policies would promote further social division, and that she was also alarmed by high unemployment, the 1981 riots, the violence of the 1984 miners' strike, and Thatcher's refusal to apply sanctions against apartheid in South Africa. Sources for the rumors included royal aide Michael Shea and Commonwealth Secretary General Ramphal Shridath, although Shea clarified that his statements were taken out of context and modified by the press. [121]Thatcher allegedly said the queen would vote for the Social Democratic Party, Thatcher's political opponents. [122]The prime minister's biographer, John Campbell, claimed that "the reports were just a piece of journalistic mischief." [123]To disprove reports of acrimony between them, Thatcher later admitted her admiration for the queen and,[124] after John Major's inauguration, Elizabeth bestowed two honors on Thatcher: the Order of Merit and the Order of the Garter. [125]

In 1987, the newly elected government in Fiji was deposed by a military coup. Isabel, as head of state, supported attempts by the governor general, *Ratu sir* Penaia Ganilau, to consolidate executive power and negotiate a settlement. The coup leader, Sitiveni Rabuka, deposed Ganilau, abolished the monarchy and declared Fiji a republic. [126]In early 1991, republican sentiment in Britain increased due to press estimates of the Queen's private wealth, which were refuted by the palace, and rumors about courtships and marital tensions in her extended family. [127]The participation of younger royals in the *It's a Royal Knockout* charity event was ridiculed,[128] and the Queen was the target of satire. [129]

1990s

In 1991, in the wake of victory in the Gulf War, Elizabeth became the first monarch to address a session of the U.S. Congress. [130]The following year, she attempted to save the marriage of her eldest son, Charles, by counseling him and his wife, Diana, to try to reconcile them. [131]

In a speech on November 24, 1992, to mark the 40th anniversary of her accession to the throne, the Queen called 1992 her *annus horribilis*, i.e., "horrible year." [6]In March, her second son, Prince Andrew, Duke of York, and his wife Sarah, separated. In April, her daughter Anne divorced her husband, Captain Mark Phillips. [132]During a state visit to Germany in October, angry demonstrators threw eggs at her in Dresden,[133] and in November Windsor Castle suffered severe damage after a devastating fire. The monarchy came under increasing criticism and public scrutiny. [134]In an unusually personal speech, Elizabeth expressed that every institution expects to receive criticism, but suggested that it should be expressed with a "touch of humor, tenderness and understanding." [135]Two days later, Prime Minister John Major announced reforms to the royal finances that had been planned since the previous year, including a first-time payment of income tax, beginning in 1993, and a reduction in the civil list. [136]In December, Charles and Diana formally separated,[137] and the year ended with the queen suing *The Sun* newspaper for copyright infringement when the text of her annual Christmas message was published two days before it was due to be broadcast. The newspaper was forced to pay legal costs and donated £200,000 to charity. [138]

In the years that followed, rumors about the marital status of Charles and Diana continued. [139]In consultation with Prime Minister Major, the Archbishop of Canterbury, George Carey, her private secretary, Robert Fellowes, and her husband, Elizabeth wrote to Charles and Diana in December 1995 saying that divorce was a desirable option. [140]A year after the divorce took place in 1996, Diana died in a car accident in Paris on August 31, 1997, at which time the queen was vacationing at Balmoral with her son and grandchildren. Diana's two sons wanted to go to church, so their grandparents took them there in the morning. [141]After a single public appearance, for five days the Queen and Duke shielded their grandchildren from intense press interest, keeping them at Balmoral, where they could mourn their mother in private;[142] however, the isolation of the royal family caused public consternation. [7]Under pressure from the hostile public reaction, the Queen returned to London and arranged a live broadcast to the world on September 5, the day before Diana's funeral. [143]In the broadcast, she expressed her admiration for her and her feelings "as grandmother" to Princes William and Henry. [144]As a result, much of the public hostility disappeared. [144]

Golden Jubilee

In 2002, Elizabeth celebrated her Golden Jubilee as Queen. Her sister and mother died in February and March respectively, [145][146] and the media speculated on whether the jubilee would be a success or a failure. [147]She again toured her kingdoms extensively, beginning in Jamaica in February, where she called the farewell banquet "memorable" after a power outage at the King's House, the governor general's official residence, plunged them into darkness. [148]As in 1977, there were street parties, commemorative events and the unveiling of monuments in honor of the occasion. One million people attended the main celebrations over three days in London,[149] and the public's enthusiasm for Elizabeth was far greater than journalists predicted. [150]

Although Elizabeth has enjoyed good health throughout her life, in 2003 she had to undergo arthroscopy on her knees and in June 2005 she suspended some engagements after catching a cold. In October 2006, she missed the opening of the Emirates Stadium due to pain caused by a contracture in her back. [151]Two months later, she was seen with a bandage on her right hand because she had been bitten by her dogs while trying to separate them when they were fighting. [152][153] In 2011, she had to cancel a religious service of the Royal Victorian Order at Windsor Castle because of a nosebleed and, consecutively, a reception because of a back injury. [154][155] In March 2013, she had to be admitted to the Edward VII Hospital because of a stomach infection with symptoms of gastroenteritis. [155]

In May 2007, *The Daily Telegraph* reported from uncredited sources that the Queen was "desperate and frustrated" by the policies of British Prime Minister Tony Blair, who had repeatedly confessed to her his concern that the British Armed Forces would be overstretched in Iraq and Afghanistan and his fears about rural issues and the countryside. [156]However, Elizabeth said she admired Blair's efforts to achieve peace in Northern Ireland. [157]On March 20, 2008, at St. Patrick's Cathedral in Armagh, the queen attended the first royal mass held outside England and Wales. [158]In 2010, she had a meeting in Scotland with Pope Benedict XVI, who recalled the deep Christian roots and values that underpin Britain and encouraged the preservation and promotion of these in the face of some "more aggressive forms of secularism" that no longer "appreciate or even tolerate" them. [159]At the invitation of Irish President Mary McAleese, in May 2011, the Queen made her first state visit to the Republic of Ireland. [160]

Elizabeth addressed the United Nations for the second time in 2010, as Queen and head of the Commonwealth of Nations. [161]Secretary-General Ban Ki-moon introduced her as an "anchor for our times." [162]During a tour of New York, followed by a visit to Canada, she officially unveiled a garden in memory of the British victims of the September 11 attacks. [162]The Queen's visit to Australia in October 2011, her 16th since 1954, was dubbed her "farewell tour" by the press due to her advanced age. [163]

Diamond Jubilee and longevity

Elizabeth's Diamond Jubilee commemorated her 60th year as Queen, with celebrations around all her realms, the wider Commonwealth of Nations. In a message released by Buckingham Palace, she stated, "In this special year, as I rededicate myself to your service, I hope we will all remember the power of togetherness and the strength of family, friendship and good neighborliness...I also hope that in this jubilee year it will become a time to give thanks for the great strides that have been made since 1952 and look to the future with clear heads and warm hearts." [164]Elizabeth and her husband undertook an extensive tour of the United Kingdom, while her children and grandchildren embarked on royal tours throughout the Commonwealth on the Queen's behalf. [165][166][167]

On June 4, Jubilee beacons were lit around the world. [168]While touring Manchester as part of her Jubilee celebrations, the Queen made a surprise appearance at a wedding party at Manchester Town Hall, which later made international news. [169]After leading a nautical parade on the River Thames aboard the Spirit of Chartwell in the company of the royal family and appearing at a concert featuring Paul McCartney, Elton John and Kylie Minogue - the most watched of the year with an average audience of 14.7 million viewers,[170]Elizabeth concluded her Diamond Jubilee celebrations on June 5, 2012 with a service at Westminster Abbey hosted by the Archbishop of Canterbury, followed by a reception at Mansion House, a procession of carriages and a balcony exit at Buckingham Palace without the presence of her husband, the Duke of Edinburgh, due to his hospitalization. [171]In November, the

Queen and her husband celebrated their blue sapphire wedding anniversary (65). [172]On December 18, 2012, the Queen became the first British sovereign to attend a peacetime cabinet meeting since George III did so in 1781. Foreign Secretary William Hague announced shortly thereafter that the part located at the southern apex of the British Antarctic Territory had been named Queen Elizabeth Land in her honor. [173]

The Queen, who opened the 1976 Olympic Games in Montreal, Canada,[174] also opened the 2012 Summer Olympics and Paralympics in London, making her the first head of state to open two Olympic Games in two countries. [175]For the London Olympics, she played herself in a short film as part of the opening ceremony, alongside Daniel Craig as James Bond. [176][177] On April 4, 2013, she received an honorary BAFTA for her patronage of the film industry and was named "most memorable Bond girl so far" at the awards ceremony. [178]On March 3, 2013, Elizabeth was admitted to King Edward VII Hospital as a precautionary measure after developing symptoms of gastroenteritis. She returned to Buckingham Palace the following day. [179]A week later, she signed the new Commonwealth Charter. [180]Due to her age and the need to limit travel, in 2013 she decided not to attend the biennial Commonwealth Heads of Government Meeting for the first time in 40 years. She was represented at the summit in Sri Lanka by Prince Charles. [181]She underwent cataract surgery in May 2018.[182] In March 2019, she opted to stop driving on public roads, largely as a result of a car accident involving her husband two months earlier. [183]

The Queen surpassed her great-great-grandmother, Queen Victoria, to become the longest reigning British monarch on December 21, 2007, and the British monarch with the longest reign and the reigning queen and head of state with the longest reign in the world on September 9, 2015.[185] [186][187] She became the oldest current monarch after King Abdullah of Saudi Arabia died on January 23, 2015.[188][189] She later became the current monarch with the longest reign and the longest serving current head of state after the death of King Bhumibol of Thailand on October 13, 2016,16, [190][191] and the longest serving current head of state after the resignation of Robert Mugabe on November 21, 2017.[192][193] On February 6, 2017, she became the first British monarch to commemorate a Sapphire Jubilee,[194] and on November 20, she was the first British monarch to celebrate a platinum wedding anniversary. [195]Philip had retired from official duties as consort to the Queen in August 2017. [196]

On April 20, 2018, Commonwealth government leaders announced that Charles would succeed her as Head of the Commonwealth. The Queen stated that it was her "sincere wish" that Charles would follow her in the role.

39

COVID-19 pandemic

On March 19, 2020, the Queen moved to Windsor Castle and secluded herself there as a precautionary measure as the COVID-19 pandemic hit the United Kingdom. [198]Public engagements were canceled and Windsor Castle followed a strict sanitary protocol dubbed "HMS Bubble." [199]On April 5, in a televised broadcast watched by some 24 million viewers in the UK,[200] asked people to "take comfort that, while we still have more to endure, better days will return." He added: "We will be with our friends again, we will be with our families again, we will meet again." [201]

On May 8, the 75th anniversary of VE Day, in a broadcast at 9 p.m., the exact time his father George VI was broadcasting in 1945, he called on people to "never give up, never despair." [202]In October, he held his first public engagement since March and visited the UK's Defense Science and Technology Laboratory to officially open its new Energy Analysis Centre. [203]On November 4, she appeared masked for the first time, during a private pilgrimage to the tomb of the Unknown Warrior in Westminster Abbey, to commemorate the centenary of his burial. [204]The same month, due to the increased risk of COVID infection, the Queen and Prince Philip returned to Windsor Castle, where they celebrated their 73rd wedding anniversary. [205]On January 9, 2021, Buckingham Palace announced that the Queen and Prince Philip had received their first dose of COVID-19 vaccine.[206] She received her second dose in April, prior to her first in-person public appearance of 2021. [207]

Philip died on April 9, 2021, making Elizabeth the first British monarch to reign as a widower or widow since Victoria. [208][209] She privately commented that his death "left a great void." [210]Due to COVID-19 restrictions, the Queen sat alone at Philip's funeral, which drew sympathy from people around the world. [211][212] Despite the pandemic, she participated in the state opening of the 2021 parliament[213] and hosted a reception for G7 leaders in Cornwall as part of the 47th G7 Summit. [214][215] On July 5, the 73rd anniversary of the founding of the NHS, she announced in a handwritten personal message that the NHS would receive the George Cross to "recognize all NHS staff, past and present, across all disciplines and in all four nations." [216]

In October 2021, Elizabeth began using a cane for comfort during public engagements for the first time since her 2004 operation.[217] On October 19, she turned down *The Oldie* award for Oldie of the Year Awards and told nominator Gyles Brandreth in a letter, "You are only as old as you feel." [218]She was briefly hospitalized on October 20, after canceling a visit to Northern Ireland for health reasons, but left the hospital the following day. [219]The hospitalization was only officially confirmed after *The Sun* published the story as a front-page exclusive. [220]The same week, he canceled his plans to travel to the COP26 summit in Glasgow following his doctor's advice to rest, and instead delivered his address via video message. [221]He was also unable to attend the 2021 National Remembrance Service after spraining his back; this was said to be unrelated to previous medical advice to rest. [222]On Nov. 21, after returning to public duties, she attended a rare joint christening of two of her great-grandchildren at the Royal Lodge in Windsor Great Park, Berkshire. [223][224] On

November 30, Barbados removed the Queen as head of state and became a republic. [225]In her Christmas 2021 broadcast, the Queen paid a personal tribute to her "beloved Philip," saying, "That mischievous, inquisitive twinkle was as bright at the end as when I first saw him." [226][227]

On February 20, 2022, Buckingham Palace announced that the Queen had tested positive for COVID-19 and was experiencing "mild cold-like symptoms." [228]Other cases were diagnosed at Windsor Castle and among relatives of the Queen. [229]The Queen canceled two virtual audiences on February 22. [230]She held a telephone conversation with the Prime Minister on February 23 amid a growing crisis on the Russian-Ukrainian border (Russia invaded Ukraine a day later). [231]On February 28, he was reported to have recovered and spent time with his family in Frogmore. [232]On March 6, it was reported that the Queen had made Windsor Castle her permanent residence and would no longer live at Buckingham Palace. [233]On March 7, the Queen had an audience with Canadian Prime Minister Justin Trudeau at Windsor Castle, which was her first in-person engagement since her COVID diagnosis. [234]She met with Canada's first indigenous governor general, Mary Simon, at Windsor Castle a week later. [235]

Platinum Jubilee

The Queen's Platinum Jubilee began on February 6, 2022.
It marks 70 years since she acceded to the throne
following the death of her father. She held a reception for
retirees, members of the local Women's Institute and
charity volunteers on the eve of the date at Sandringham
House. [236]In her Accession Day message, Elizabeth
renewed her lifetime commitment to public service, which
she originally made in 1947. [237]

On March 14, the Queen was unable to attend the annual
Commonwealth Day service; which had a special focus on
her Platinum Jubilee year. [238]However, it was reported that
this was due to mobility issues rather than health-related
problems, and the Prince of Wales represented her at the
service. [239][240]

He has no intention of abdicating,[241] although the
proportion of public duties performed by Prince Charles
has increased as Elizabeth reduces her commitments.
[242][243][244]

Public perceptions and criticisms

Queen Elizabeth rarely gives interviews and little is known of her personal views. As a parliamentary monarch, she has not expressed her political views in a public forum. She has a deep sense of religious and civil duty, and takes her coronation oath very seriously. [245]Apart from her religious role as head of the Church of England, she maintains an excellent relationship with her church and the Church of Scotland. [246]

He met with leaders of other religions, in addition to granting his personal patronage to the Council of Christians and Jews. [247]

In his annual Christmas message to the Commonwealth of Nations, he often offers insights into his faith, as in the year 2000, when he spoke about the theological significance of the new millennium marking the 2000th anniversary of the birth of Jesus Christ:

Elizabeth is patron of more than 600 charities and other organizations. [249]Her main hobbies are horseback riding and dogs, especially her Corgis. [250]Her wardrobe generally consists of solid-colored coats and decorative hats, which allow her to be easily spotted in a crowd. [251]

In the 1950s, as a young woman at the beginning of her reign, Elizabeth was depicted as a glamorous "fairy tale queen." [252]After the trauma of war, there was a time of hope, heralding a period of progress and achievement known as the "new Elizabethan era." [253]Lord Altrincham's 1957 accusation that her speeches sounded like those of a "pedantic schoolgirl" was considered extremely rare. [254]In the late 1960s, the documentary *Royal Family* and the television broadcast of Charles's investiture as Prince of Wales were the result of her attempts to present a more modern image of the monarchy. [255]

At her silver jubilee in 1977, the crowds and celebrations were indeed enthusiastic,[256] but public criticism of the royal family in the 1980s increased as the personal and work lives of Elizabeth's children came under scrutiny in the media. [257]Elizabeth's popularity declined considerably in the 1990s. Pressured by public opinion, she began paying income tax for the first time and Buckingham Palace opened its doors to the public. [258]The dissatisfaction of the British monarchy reached its peak with Diana's death, although Elizabeth's popularity was regained after the message broadcast live on September 5, 1997. [259]

In November 1999, in a referendum in Australia on the future of the monarchy, the preference was for its permanence rather than an indirectly elected head of state. [260]Polls in Britain in 2006 and 2007 revealed widespread support for Elizabeth,[261] and referendums in Tuvalu in 2008 and St. Vincent and the Grenadines in 2009 rejected proposals to abolish the monarchy. [262]

Finance

According to an agreement dating from the first half of the 18th century, the Crown's assets were transferred to the State, in exchange for a fixed income. Elizabeth II's personal fortune has been the subject of speculation for many years. In 2010, *Forbes* magazine estimated her net worth to be around $450 million,[263] although official statements from Buckingham Palace in 1993 expressed that estimates of £100 million were "grossly exaggerated." [264]Jock Colville estimated his fortune at £2 million in 1971 (the rough equivalent of £21 million today). [265note 2] The Royal Collection, which includes works of art and Crown jewels, is not the Queen's personal property and is held in trusts,[266] as are the residences at Buckingham Palace, Windsor Castle[267] and the Duchy of Lancaster, an investment portfolio valued at £383 million in 2011.[268] Sandringham House and Balmoral Castle, on the other hand, are the Queen's private holdings. [267]The British Crown Estate - with holdings of 7.3 million pounds in 2011 -[269] is held in trust by the nation and cannot be sold or belong to the Queen. [270]

Valuation and influence

According to some, her reign has been characterized by a major national unification effort, through which Elizabeth II has been responsible for maintaining and preventing the separation of the United Kingdom from its constituent countries, although not a single public initiative of the queen in this regard is known. In addition, the monarch, as head of the Commonwealth of Nations, managed a genuine transition from an imperial system to a free association of nations,[271] in which mutual cooperation, democracy and cultural exchange are its main purposes. The sovereign has played considerable roles during the various administrations of her prime ministers, through her election of heads of government and the preservation of the stability and political continuity of the United Kingdom. [272]

Despite the limited political role to which the British monarchy was reduced after World War II, essentially limited to symbolic acts, and the changes that took place in the relationship with the former colonies, Queen Elizabeth II sought to preserve the unifying character of the Crown in the political space of the former empire, which became the Commonwealth after decolonization. [273][274]

Her visions of the monarchy and the way she has gradually transformed this institution into one more compatible with the 21st century have made her the paradigm of European monarchs, whose statesmanship is often imitated by numerous heads of state. Elizabeth II was chosen "person of the year" by *Time magazine* in 1952 and, according to

Forbes, is the eighth richest leader in the world with a fortune estimated at 450 million dollars. [275]

In popular culture

Elizabeth was parodied during the 1980s in the television series *Spitting Image* and in 2006 was played by actress Helen Mirren in *The Queen*, a film directed by Stephen Frears, which recounts the Queen's reaction to the death of Lady Di in 1997.[276] In 2010 she was played by the young Freya Wilson in *The King's Speech* (winner of four Oscars, with Colin Firth and Geoffrey Rush). [277]In the popular television series *The Simpsons*, she was featured as a guest star in some episodes such as *The Regina Monologues*, *To Surveil With Love* and *The Simpsons 138th Episode Spectacular*. He has also appeared on numerous banknotes and coins of different countries: United Kingdom, Canada, Australia, New Zealand, Fiji, Barbados, Bahamas, Belize, as well as Bermuda, Falkland Islands, Cayman Islands, Eastern Caribbean, Gibraltar, Guernsey, Isle of Man, Jersey and St. Helena. The postage stamps of the United Kingdom do not bear the name of the country, but the effigy of the Queen.

Treatments, titles and weapons

Titles

Elizabeth II has obtained titles throughout her life: first as granddaughter and daughter of kings, then by marriage (such as Duchess of Edinburgh or Countess of Merioneth) and finally as sovereign. Officially, she has a different title in each of her kingdoms: Queen of Canada in Canada, Queen of Australia in Australia, etc. In the Channel Islands and Isle of Man, which are Crown dependencies and do not belong to the United Kingdom, she is recognized as *Duke* (duke) of Normandy and *Lord* (lord) of Man respectively, and in Fiji as *supreme head* by the Great Council of Chiefs, without constitutional powers, as Fiji is a republic, until the dissolution of this institution in 2012. Other traditional titles are Defender of the Faith and *Duke* of Lancaster. [272]

Officially her title in the United Kingdom is: *Elizabeth the Second, by the Grace of God, Queen of the United Kingdom of Great Britain and Northern Ireland, and of her other Realms and Territories, Head of the Commonwealth of Nations, Defender of the Faith.* [279]

Coat of arms and banners

In 1944,[280] Elizabeth's coat of arms consisted of a losange (lozenge) containing the coat of arms of the United Kingdom, differentiated with a lambel of three argent-colored pendants: in the first and third pendant was the cross of St. George and in the center a Tudor rose. [281]As Duchess of Edinburgh was added the ribbon of the Order of the Garter. After her ascension to the throne in 1952, she adopted another coat of arms: the full arms of the sovereign.

His standard as monarch consists of a flag divided into four quarters: in the first and fourth quarters are the elements of the coat of arms of England: three lions passant of gold on a field of gules (red). In the second, representing Scotland, a lion rampant within a double trechor with heraldic flowers, on a field of gold. In the third quadrant, for Northern Ireland, a harp of gold on a field of azure is represented. In the constituent nation of Scotland, the standard varies in its quarters: the Scottish lion rampant appears in the first and fourth quarters, and that of England in the second. The Queen also has personal flags in other countries: Australia, Canada, New Zealand, Jamaica and Barbados. [282]

Family

Together with her husband, the Duke of Edinburgh, the Queen had four children: Charles, Anne, Andrew and Edward. In addition, the couple has eight grandchildren and twelve great-grandchildren.

- Charles, Prince of Wales (born November 14, 1948), is the heir to the British Crown. He married Diana, Princess of Wales (1961-1997) on July 29, 1981, with whom he had two sons: William of Cambridge and Henry of Sussex. He divorced Diana on August 28, 1996. On April 9, 2005 he married in second marriage, in a civil ceremony, with Camilla, Duchess of Cornwall.
    - William, Duke of Cambridge (born June 21, 1982), married Catherine Middleton, now known as Catherine, Duchess of Cambridge (born January 9, 1982), on April 29, 2011. He is second in line to the British throne.
        - Prince George of Cambridge (born July 22, 2013). Since his birth, he has been third in line to the British throne.
        - Princess Charlotte of Cambridge (born May 2, 2015).
        - Prince Louis of Cambridge (born April 23, 2018).
    - Prince Henry, Duke of Sussex (born September 15, 1984), married Meghan Markle, currently known as Meghan,

Duchess of Sussex (born August 4, 1981), on May 19, 2018.

- Archie Mountbatten-Windsor (born May 6, 2019).
- Lilibet Mountbatten-Windsor (born June 4, 2021).

- Anne, Princess Royal (born August 15, 1950), married Captain Mark Phillips (born September 22, 1948) on November 14, 1973, and had two children, Peter Phillips and Zara Phillips. She divorced on April 28, 1992. Her second marriage took place on December 12, 1992 to Vice Admiral *Sir* Timothy Laurence (born March 1, 1955).
  - Peter Phillips (born November 15, 1977), married Autumn Patricia Kelly (born May 3, 1978) on May 17, 2008. He divorced on June 14, 2021.
    - Savannah Phillips (born December 29, 2010).
    - Isla Phillips (born March 29, 2012).
  - Zara Tindall (born May 15, 1981), married Michael James Tindall (born October 18, 1978) on July 30, 2011.
    - Mia Tindall (born January 17, 2014).
    - Lena Tindall (born June 18, 2018).
    - Lucas Tindall (born March 21, 2021).
- Andrew, Duke of York (born February 19, 1960), married Sarah, Duchess of York (born October 15, 1959), mother of his two daughters, Beatrice and Eugenie, on July 23, 1986. He divorced on May 30, 1996.

- Princess Beatrice of York (born August 8, 1988). She married Edoardo Mapelli Mozzi on July 17, 2020 (born November 19, 1983).
  - Sienna Mapelli Mozzi (born September 18, 2021).
- Princess Eugenie of York (born March 23, 1990). She married Jack Brooksbank on October 12, 2018 (born May 3, 1986).
  - August Brooksbank (born February 9, 2021).

- Edward, Earl of Wessex (born March 10, 1964), married Sophia, Countess of Wessex (born January 20, 1965) on June 19, 1999, with whom he has two children.
  - Lady Louise Mountbatten-Windsor (born November 8, 2003).
  - James Mountbatten-Windsor, Viscount Severn (born December 17, 2007).

CPSIA information can be obtained
at www.ICGtesting.com
Printed in the USA
BVHW032242250922
647977BV00016B/403